GETTING TO KNOW
THE U.S. PRESIDENTS

JOHN QUINCY
ADAMS

SIXTH PRESIDENT
1825 – 1829

WRITTEN AND ILLUSTRATED BY MIKE VENEZIA

CHILDREN'S PRESS®
A DIVISION OF SCHOLASTIC INC.
NEW YORK   TORONTO   LONDON   AUCKLAND   SYDNEY
MEXICO CITY   NEW DELHI   HONG KONG
DANBURY, CONNECTICUT

Reading Consultant: Nanci R. Vargus, Ed.D., Assistant Professor, School of Education, University of Indianapolis

Historical Consultant: Marc J. Selverstone, Ph.D., Assistant Professor, Miller Center of Public Affairs, University of Virginia

Photographs © 2004:
Art Resource, NY: 32 (National Portrait Gallery, Smithsonian Institution, Washington, D.C.), 30 (Reunion des Musees Nationaux)
Bridgeman Art Library International Ltd., London/New York/New-York Historical Society, New York, USA: 29
Brown Brothers: 4 bottom, 6
Corbis Images: 4 top (Bettmann), 28 (Geoffrey Clements), 17 (Gianni Dagli Orti), 3 (The Corcoran Gallery of Art), 24
North Wind Picture Archives: 9, 20
PictureHistory.com: 18 left, 19
Stock Montage, Inc.: 26
Superstock, Inc.: 13 (Anatoly Sapronenkov), 12

Colorist for illustrations: Dave Ludwig

Library of Congress Cataloging-in-Publication Data

Venezia, Mike.
  John Quincy Adams / written and illustrated by Mike Venezia.
    p. cm. — (Getting to know the U.S. presidents)
Summary: An introduction to the life of John Quincy Adams, son of the second president who himself became the sixth president.
  ISBN 0-516-22611-8 (lib. bdg.)   0-516-27480-5 (pbk.)
  1. Adams, John Quincy, 1767-1848—Juvenile literature. 2. Presidents—United States—Biography—Juvenile literature. [1. Adams, John Quincy, 1767-1848. 2. Presidents.] I. Title. II. Series.
  E377.V46 2003
  973.5'5'092—dc22

                              2003015961

17 16 15 R 17 16 15
                              113

A portrait of John Quincy Adams by George Peter Alexander Healy (The Corcoran Gallery of Art, Washington, D.C.)

John Quincy Adams was the sixth president of the United States. He was born in 1767 in Braintree, Massachusetts. John Quincy grew up in just the right family for someone who wanted to become a president. He learned a lot from his father, John Adams, who was the second president of the United States.

A portrait of John Adams, the father of John Quincy Adams

John Quincy Adams pretty much took after his father. Both of the Adamses were very serious, stubborn, impatient, and cranky a lot of the time. They got their way by never giving up on the ideas they believed in.

A photograph of John Quincy Adams in 1848

Because of their attitudes, these two men didn't have many close friends. Neither of them got elected for a second term after serving one term as president.

THE BIRTH PLACES OF JOHN AND JOHN QUINCY ADAMS
at Quincy Mass.

An engraving showing the birthplace of John Quincy Adams in Braintree (now Quincy), Massachusetts

Luckily, most of the ideas John Quincy Adams had were good ones. They had to do with making sure people's rights were protected and with helping the young United States grow into a stronger country.

John Quincy didn't have a very normal childhood. Even at the age of five, he felt responsible for taking care of his family while his father was away on long business trips.

When John Quincy started his education, it wasn't at the local school. Assistants from his father's law office became his teachers. John Quincy was very smart. He quickly learned the subjects of ancient history and Latin.

While John Quincy Adams was growing up, Massachusetts was one of thirteen colonies in North America that were owned by Great Britain and the King of England. King George III insisted on forcing colonists to pay more and more taxes as time went on.

Colonists wanted to have a say in whether they should have to pay any new taxes. King George and the British government, though, didn't care what the colonists thought. Finally, the colonists became so angry that they decided to break away from England and start their own country.

Like these colonists in Boston, John Quincy Adams and his mother watched the Battle of Bunker Hill from a distance.

When John Quincy Adams was eight years old, the Revolutionary War began. It was a scary time. John Quincy and his mother even watched a fierce battle from a hilltop near their home.

In 1778, Mr. Adams was asked to travel to Europe to see if France would help the United States with their fight for freedom. Even though travel by sea could be dangerous, Mr. Adams thought the trip would be a good experience for his ten-year-old son. John Quincy's mother was especially worried, but finally agreed to let her son go.

During the voyage, John Quincy's ship was chased by British warships. The ship also ran into a terrible storm, and even attacked and captured a British cargo boat! In the middle of all that excitement, John Quincy took time to learn the French language.

John Quincy Adams and his father finally arrived safely in Europe. John Quincy attended the best schools there. He learned some foreign languages as well as other difficult subjects. Most of his teachers agreed that he was a genius.

A map of Europe and Russia in the late 1700s

A painting showing St. Petersburg, Russia, in the early 1800s

In 1782, when John Quincy was fourteen years old, an American diplomat asked him to be his assistant in St. Petersburg, Russia. A diplomat represents his or her country and tries to get important business done with the governments of other countries. Even though John Quincy was only fourteen, he was as smart and skilled as any adult. So at an early age, John Quincy Adams began to serve his country.

John Quincy was bothered by what he saw in Russia. It seemed like everyone there was either very, very rich, or very, very poor. Poor people struggled almost like slaves their whole lives, working in farm fields and at other hard jobs. They never had enough to eat and had to wear raggedy clothes all the time.

After spending seven years in Europe, John Quincy returned home. By that time, the United States had won its war with Britain and had officially become its own nation. John was thankful. Unlike the people in Russia, he would be free to choose the way he wanted to live his life. John Quincy finished up his education at Harvard College in Cambridge, Massachusetts. After graduation, he became a lawyer.

John Quincy Adams became a lawyer to please his father. His heart was never really in it, though. John Quincy was really much more interested in learning about the new United States government. He began writing clever newspaper articles that supported the way the nation's first president, George Washington, was doing his job.

John Quincy Adams moved to The Hague (above) when President George Washington appointed him U.S. minister to the Netherlands in 1794.

President Washington appreciated John Quincy's reports and offered him a job as a United States diplomat in the Netherlands. John Adams, who was vice president at the time, was very proud of his son.

A portrait of John Quincy Adams in 1796 by John Singleton Copley

In 1794, John Quincy Adams left for the Netherlands. It was the first of many foreign countries he would go to as a representative of the United States. John Quincy used his earlier experiences and his knowledge of different languages to solve problems and create friendships with foreign governments.

Once, when he was visiting England, he fell in love with the daughter of a wealthy family who lived in London. After dating for a while, Louisa Catherine Johnson and John Quincy decided to get married.

A portrait of Louisa Catherine Johnson around the time of her marriage to John Quincy Adams

An illustration showing Brittish sailors kidnapping U.S. sailors in 1807

John Quincy returned to Massachusetts with Louisa in 1801. Soon after they arrived, John Quincy was appointed to represent his state as a U.S. senator.

At this time, the United States still had some serious problems with England. The English navy kept stopping American ships and forcing sailors to join their side.

Thomas Jefferson was president of the United States at the time. In 1807, he called for an embargo, or stoppage of trade, with England. President Jefferson hoped the embargo would teach the English a lesson so they would stop their dangerous and insulting behavior.

John Quincy Adams agreed with President Jefferson, but people from Massachusetts hated the idea of an embargo. They made lots of money by doing business with England. Suddenly, people who had wanted John Quincy to be their senator became so angry that they forced him out of his job.

John Quincy Adams was disappointed but felt that protecting American sailors was more important than being senator. Even though John Quincy knew he was risking his job, he refused to back down from what he thought was right.

Although some people were angry with John Quincy, many others respected his point of view. After losing his job as senator, he went on to become a successful diplomat to Russia and Great Britain. He then became secretary of state under President James Monroe.

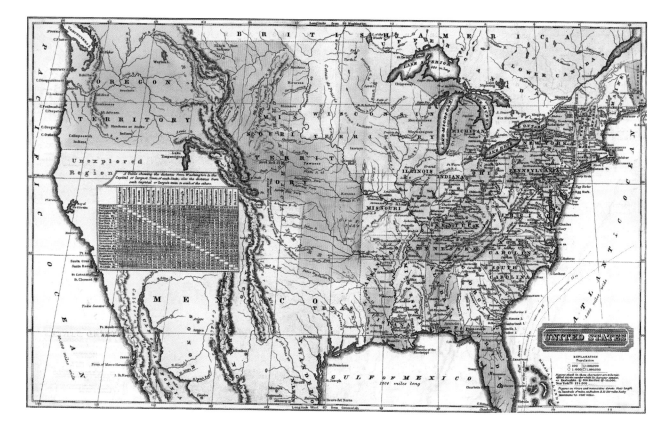

This map shows how the United States looked in the 1820s, a few years after Secretary of State John Quincy Adams helped acquire Florida from Spain.

As secretary of state, John Quincy got a lot of important things done. He helped the United States buy Florida from Spain. He also helped work out where the borders for the new United States would be. John Quincy helped write the Monroe Doctrine, too. This important document warned European nations not to try to start up any new colonies in North or South America.

An illustration showing Andrew Jackson (on white horse) during the Battle of New Orleans

John Quincy Adams decided to run for president in 1824 after James Monroe's term was over. He barely won the election against Andrew Jackson. General Jackson was a popular war hero who had led the famous Battle of New Orleans at the end of the War of 1812.

Members of the government who had supported Andrew Jackson were really angry that he lost. Right away they started saying things about President Adams that weren't very nice. They promised to make his time as president as difficult as possible!

The Rocky Mountains, shown here in a painting by Albert Bierstadt, were part of the magnificent lands to the west of the quickly growing United States of the early 1800s.

The United States was growing quickly during the time John Quincy Adams was president. President Adams wanted to help. He suggested using U.S. government money to build more new roads, bridges, and canals. He thought it would be a good idea to also build observatories across the country for the scientific study of stars and planets.

President Adams wanted the army and navy to grow bigger and stronger, too. Unfortunately, Andrew Jackson's friends and other members of Congress blocked almost every idea the president came up with. Building and expanding the nation's canal system was one of the few things President Adams was able to get done.

To encourage trade and help strengthen the nation, President Adams wanted to build more canals like the Erie Canal (above), which opened in 1825.

A painting of the White House in the 1820s, by Jefferson Vail (Musée de la cooperation franco-americaine, Blerancourt, France)

John Quincy Adams had a pretty miserable time as president. He had a lot of good ideas but wasn't able to get anyone interested in them. This was partly his own fault. John Quincy was too serious and unfriendly, and he only wanted to do things his way. Members of the Senate and House of Representatives weren't willing to help him very much.

Andrew Jackson's friends kept giving John Quincy a hard time, too.

But these weren't his only problems. On warm summer mornings, President Adams liked to swim in the Potomac River—in the nude. Once someone stole all his clothes from the riverbank!

An illustration showing John Quincy Adams collapsing in the House of Representatives in 1848 (National Portrait Gallery, Smithsonian Institution, Washington, D.C.)

John Quincy Adams lost the next election to Andrew Jackson. He went back home to retire, but the people of Massachusetts soon asked him to be a representative in Congress.

John Quincy was happy to serve his country again. For eighteen years he fought for his beliefs, arguing as hard as he could to convince people that slavery was wrong. Near the end of his life, John Quincy Adams was considered an American hero.

In 1848, at the age of eighty, John Quincy Adams collapsed at his desk in the House of Representatives. When he died two days later, even his enemies were saddened.